Haiku Avenue

333 haiku poems

by

Robert Hobkirk

Copyright

Haiku Avenue: 333 haiku poems

Copyright © 2015 by Robert Hobkirk

All rights are reserved. This includes the right to reproduce any portion of this book in any form.

Self-published with CreateSpace by Robert Hobkirk

First printing in February, 2015

ISBN-13: 978-1508457435

ISBN-10: 1508457433

Dedication

This book is dedicated to Jeannine Hobkirk, my loving wife. Jeannine worked diligently, counting syllables, finding grammar and spelling glitches, and with fresh eyes reminding me from time to time, "this doesn't make any sense."

Introduction

Introduction:

I wrote these haiku poems from September 2014 through January 2015 in what may not have been a creative storm, but at least a creative heavy mist. My first intention was to write a book with 365 haikus. This would imply a poem a day. I had written 365 poems but decided on 333 instead. It had nothing to do with the superstition of certain numbers being lucky or having certain powers. For me 333 was a more interesting number, more poetic, so I culled the weaker poems and kept the stronger.

All of the poems are in the classical Japanese style of seventeen syllables, three lines of 5-7-5 syllables. Sticking with the classical style was a help in trying to crystalize the poem into a poignant vision rather than just writing a short poem, having it wander off into more words and syllables. By not saying it all, the reader can fill the unsaid in with his or her imagination and participate with the creation. To see what lies in a clear stream doesn't take imagination, but to see what may lie in a muddy river does.

Some of these poems are written about the classical haiku subject – nature and the season, or reference to the season. Since most of these poems were written in the fall and winter, it's no surprise that there are poems about this time of year. Some of these poems aren't classical in subject, but modern American city life, relationships, even the economy. If the inspiration for the poem wasn't

Introduction

presently happening, it was a memory. Some memories when we recall them become short stories, and others are haikus.

Robert Hobkirk

1.

Thimble full of hope

wooden match struck against stone

every thing begins.

2.

Hard rain after dark

we slept in a driftwood hut

ocean snored all night.

3

Hard working women

baristas make very good wives

they know how to smile.

Haiku Avenue

4.

Bright shiny trout lures

fluorescent pink Power Bait

fishermen catchers.

5.

White plates clattering

Steaks sizzling on frying pan

take time to listen.

6.

Rocky stream roaring

bird chattering at first gray light

cabin sits silent.

7.

Morning first coffee

both hands holding warm round cup

time to give up thanks.

8.

Gypsies on the street

begging for a small handout

pigeons work for crumbs.

9.

Tumbling colors

looking through kaleidoscope

beauty born again.

Haiku Avenue

10.

Watching train at night

sparks light up the screeching wheels

silence brings up rear.

11.

I picked up a toad

careful not to be peed on

he blinked his dull eyes.

12.

Late afternoon nap

dogs, old men rest together

cats, women work on.

13.

Finally the sun

shadows come out for a walk -

bright geraniums.

14.

Empty cardboard box

hunkered down for the long night

rain drops on the roof.

15.

Squirrels chattering

still feels like summer to me

putting nuts in bank.

Haiku Avenue

16.

Chick falls out of nest

red ants tug and pull on bird

they will not give up.

17.

A change in season

hunting catalogs arrive -

teal first to fly south.

18.

Off to dead end job

fat traffic jam on freeway

sleep a little more.

19.

Way back in the day

hot water bottle in bed

four feet kept toasty.

20.

Hatchet chopping block

Grandma is cooking chicken

no stains on apron.

21.

Kids with glowing hands

fire flies in mayonnaise jars

big dipper above.

Haiku Avenue

22.

Half glass of water

on stand silently reminds

don't forget your meds.

23.

Wake up and give thanks

boot up computer with switch

connect to power.

24.

Macho garbage truck

growls, squeals, rattles, whistles, rolls

wild new age street band.

25.

My Dad built houses

I swing the hammer and miss

bent nail laughs at me.

26.

Turning on light

rat runs across living room

burglar caught in act.

27.

Billionaire quoted

words on empty coffee cups -

recycle or trash?

28.

Candy in the street

one day after Halloween

mouthful of Skittles.

29.

Lonely old grave yard

only one grave has flowers.

Who is left to care?

30.

A perfect balance

peanut butter and jelly

rich and poor love it.

31.

Turtle out walking

down the black asphalt highway

lost or exploring?

32.

San Bernardino

Hell's Angels, McDonald's Burgers

made in U.S.A.

33.

Late Sunday morning

need to congregate again

Church of Saint Starbucks.

34.

Voices above in sky

geese flying in the dark night –

look up see dim stars.

35.

Medical Center

two old women in wheel chairs

where is family?

36.

Before sun came up

three coyotes yodeling

at sun rise, birds sang.

Robert Hobkirk

37.

Hard acorns falling

filling the house eve gutters

climb ladder don't fall.

38.

We get to heaven

going through our tough lives

we will understand.

39.

December fishing

hook and bait drop down through ice

perch flops in white snow.

Haiku Avenue

40.

Sugar hangover

wasting the zombie morning

blind man taps his cane.

41.

. Conductor punches ticket

how does he remember faces

he forgets birthdays.

42.

Snail travels slowly

eyes up high always on watch

laughing kids scare him.

43.

Find faithful husband

you have found something special –

good ground ploughs easy.

44.

Baked chicken carcass

wrestle over the wishbone –

heart's secret desire.

45.

Beads of morning dew

sun dries invisible web

spider waits on edge.

Haiku Avenue

46.

We amused ourselves

hand shadows on bedroom wall

barking dogs chasing.

47.

Lightning crackles night

heavy black thunder shakes house

dogs hide under porch.

48.

Warm Michigan nights

we caught fireflies in jars

they died by morning.

49.

Bikes on city streets

watch your step even on green –

mad wasps will sting you.

50.

Don't shoot, they're not geese

tundra swan falling to ground –

man lives with regret.

51.

Cranes feeding in fields

morning mist like a prayer shawl

Africa calling.

Haiku Avenue

52.

Wires overhead

no smoke from electric train

solar will power.

53.

Cat creeping by creek

looks over shoulder at me

guilty look on face.

54.

Crop duster strafes field

poison cloud falls killing bugs.

What will pheasants eat?

55.

Amsterdam morning

people in the dark on bikes

mysterious folk.

56.

Happy folks I knew

satisfied with all they had –

greed brings discontent.

57.

Gray day sun rising

Frankfurt businessmen wound up –

be still drink your tea.

Haiku Avenue

58.

Listen to German

everyone yapping orders –

remember drill sergeant?

59.

Artist spends his time

others have no time to waste –

fish breathes in water.

60.

Tourist drags suitcase

down ancient cobblestone street

thump, thump, wheel falls off.

Robert Hobkirk

61.

Wipers on windshield

reminding me I'm lazy

screech, scratch, screech, scratch, screech.

62.

Red green and gold bike

gun rack on bull handle bars

single speed no brakes.

63.

Dog on steady point

snow crunching under my boots

cackling explosion.

Haiku Avenue

64.

Long lines everywhere

folks hate to stand still for long

time to think things through.

65.

Jay street is dark with rain

neon raven flapping wings

flashing rain puddle.

66.

Father wore cologne

my Dad was a carpenter

he smelled like lumber.

Robert Hobkirk

67.

Saturate my soul

everyone I meet loves me –

old jar holds honey.

68.

Pushing turtle off

gangster duck waddles on log

no revenge is planned.

69.

Yellow daffodils

planted by freeway onramp -

motorcycle cop.

Haiku Avenue

70.

Gray gypsy lady

euro coin dropped in cup

now good luck returns.

71.

Plums fall from branches

one or two picked up by birds

dropped and sprout next Spring.

72.

High heels clicking time

mercy, she casts a dark spell

bad times are coming.

Robert Hobkirk

73.

Noisy kids leave train

beautiful quiet returns

man shouts in cell phone.

74.

Sitting on toilet

watching earwig walk across

vanishes in crack.

75.

Night's darkness lifted

morning fog was everywhere

silver sun rising.

Haiku Avenue

76.

Trains and coffee shops

meditation stimulation

poet finds a corner.

77.

Our cat was calico

we gave her food, clean water

we gave her no name.

78.

Ultramarine blue

burnt sienna plus lead white

gray sky, gray water.

79.

The barista said

one hundred different cups –

I enjoy our talks.

80.

One red wing black bird

lands and rests on brown cattail

sways once back and forth.

81.

Car lights, wipers on

good for nothing soupy fog

farm fields groan for rain.

82.

With big sharp talons

owl hung up in star thistle

she waves me over.

83.

White lazy sun

cathedral piercing gray skies

train pulls into Delft.

84.

Salmon making run

stepping stones across clear stream

barking dog on bank.

Robert Hobkirk

85.

Baited hook smells sweet

shark tattoo swims on shoulder

man dives overboard.

86.

Having a bad day

grumpy lady in kiosk

made her smile with smile.

87.

After I'm buried

this tree will go on growing.

Will it remember?

Haiku Avenue

88.

Almost every day

I hear the same woodpecker

rapping the same tune.

89.

Vienna drizzle

shelter in the museum

dry art on the walls.

90.

Starbucks coffee shop

just enough toilet paper

one more small blessing.

Robert Hobkirk

91.

Geese flying high up

shotgun brings down one feather

flock keeps rowing south.

92.

Car stopped on red light

hail hammers windshield and roof

green takes forever.

93.

One dead coyote

hanging on barbed wire fence

good thief Saint Dimas.

94.

Freezing cold weather

silenced the mountain blue lake

with crystal clear ice.

95.

So many strangers

dreadful loneliness in street

ambulance wails on.

96.

Grape vines on hillside

arms stretched out on wire and wood

bright ribbons flashing.

Robert Hobkirk

97.

Bar door wide open

outside, pot belly man smokes

red-white-and-blue flaps.

98.

Down muddy river

summer straw hat floats on by

red ribbon bright band.

99.

Get up for the new day

bath room shower, shave, shampoo

hear birds, lie back down.

100.

Steel wheels on steel tracks

iron violins screeching

train rings friendly bell.

101.

Starlight and shadows

Venus low on horizon

bull bellows love call.

102.

How do butterflies

migrate over continents?

They fly together.

103.

If a butterfly

knew how far the journey was,

never would begin.

104.

Chess is so Russian

brooding patience forever

suffering virtue.

105.

Neon sign in store

blasts out "alkohole" in red.

Poles say what they think.

Haiku Avenue

106.

How does he hold on?

Bumblebee on car windshield

stop at light, he's gone.

107.

Dusty rug on line,

boy beats rug with baseball bat

time out – dust in eye.

108.

I look in the sky

geese, swans, ducks should be flying south

blank sky disappoints.

109.

Cutting out comics

taping them on fridge's door

laughs rise like incense.

110.

Cows grazing on grass

all headed in a circle

perfectly calm day.

111.

Temptation creeping

cigarette devil knocking

don't answer the door.

Haiku Avenue

112.

Seven days after

New Year's Day Resolution

sugar cube melting.

113.

Brown cow in pasture

with an extra set of legs

calf stands by her side.

114.

Wake up one morning

rain barrel overflowing

creative flash flood.

115.

Women get on bus

I listen to their Polish –

grandma memories.

116.

Have not seen for years

laundry basket heaping clothes

colors on a line.

117.

Rock thrown in still pond

ripples last only seconds

flowers wilt on grave.

118.

Throw a flat round stone

mud hen runs on loud water

skipping across pond.

119.

January fields

wild geese resting in delta

leave before tractors.

120.

Pink sky, orange sun down

treat to end a lonely day

I look up, it's gone.

121.

Geese flying across

pink horizon hanging on

night closes curtain.

122.

I prayed for healing

my dad's body got sicker

light shined out from him.

123.

Into café walks

man with cane, wife with walker

we think – never us.

Haiku Avenue

124.

Hot sun on window

house fly buzzing up and down

small hole in screen door.

125.

Caged wild animals

insanity on their faces

no work drives men nuts.

126.

Refrigerator

door swings open and closes

burn out light, never.

Robert Hobkirk

127.

Baby crab on beach

walking sideways with claws raised

seagull pokes and jabs.

128.

Fish and chips café

elbows on greasy table

few people eating.

129.

Pomegranate tree

when will it bare red ripe fruit –

good things grow slowly.

130.

Old persimmon tree

loses leaves every winter

blossoms every spring.

131.

Old dog sleeps away

chasing pheasants in his dreams.

Will we hunt again?

132.

Standing in porch light

snow falling down from black sky

her car drives away.

133.

Swimming in water

mayonnaise jar with tadpoles

water starts to smell.

134.

Brown standing water

pollywogs swimming in ditch

boy kneels on the bank.

135.

Running through the woods

my black beagle named Lady

chasing cottontails.

136.

Boo it's Halloween

hurry darkness bring the ghosts

next day smashed pumpkins.

137.

Saturday morning

everyone is out walking

dogs love Saturdays.

138.

Twenty years to life

his honor was in bad mood

leg irons clang away.

139.

Soft running water

rounds off the jagged edge –

a smile makes a friend.

140.

Taking fishing break

blue heron standing on log –

stomach full, why work.

141.

Morning coffee break

banana not a doughnut –

small changes brings change.

Haiku Avenue

142.

Crabs stranded on shore

pushed up by the gray spring tide

washed up on my bed.

143.

Veterans' Day morning

standing in line for coffee

hurry up and wait.

144.

Flying sandhill cranes

down the Great Central Valley

landing in rice field.

145.

Speckled belly geese

gleaning rice left on chopped field

morning mist rising.

146.

Sunflowers growing

in California farm field

all facing same way.

147.

My mouth open wide

white snow falling from gray sky

catch snow flake on tongue.

Haiku Avenue

148.

Picking blackberries,

my fingers got stained purple.

Thorns pierced my Levis.

149.

Night rain wind howling

oak tree falls in flooded creek

bird nest floats down stream.

150.

Out on the mud flats

digging for clams with shovel

mud plays tug of war.

151.

Ship in the harbor

loads up with rice for China

crane swings back and forth.

152.

Striped bass frenzy feed

chase a school of silver shad

water boils, then calm.

153.

Scotts tried baking bread

did not throw failure away

failed tough bread named scones.

154.

Small Asian girls hunched

manicuring nails in shop

black hair hanging down.

155.

Leaf blowers blasting

leaves doing cartwheels in air

silence comes, leaves rest.

156.

Painting house with wife

practice not biting head off

one more gentle coat.

Robert Hobkirk

157.

Some have gentle voice

other people only screech –

doves and crows in tree.

158.

Sometimes on death beds

the dying hear angry words

difficult living.

159.

Empty baseball field

baseball is gone until spring

radio is silent.

160.

White heron fishing

statue standing on creek bank

hiding fish come out.

161.

In the horse corral

small quail scratched for fallen feed.

A mare stomped her hoof.

162.

My dog stuck his head

into the berry bramble.

The rabbit refused.

Robert Hobkirk

163.

Muskrat swims close by.

I move and he dives under –

today disappears.

164.

Not even a breeze

still pond is gently disturbed

rain drops on water.

165.

San Francisco night

lonely fog horn calling low.

Your mouth tastes like mint.

166.

In old Amsterdam

behind the old train station

big water harbor.

167.

Walking along the shore

small cold waves run in and out.

Dead fish rises and falls.

168.

Green maple tree seeds

falling from branches above,

scattered on asphalt.

169.

Lightning hits old bridge

reflection flashes water

barge passes under.

170.

Floating down river

log passes by iron bridge

out into the bay.

171.

Green wing teal over

decoys on quiet water

shotgun kills silence.

Haiku Avenue

172.

Tornado on shore

great lake with choppy water

we row to harbor.

173.

Boiling with color

thunderheads over Detroit

summer shouts again.

174.

Geese flying in night

between earth and crescent moon

wind rattles corn stalks.

175.

Silver shad for bait

cast out and don't mess with it –

patience fills basket.

176.

California sun

dark green leaves, bright orange ripe fruit

at end of alley.

177.

Hard work builds big house

laziness can burn it down –

small match makes big fire.

178.

Sparrows are lucky

ordinary brown feathers –

no sparrows in cage.

179.

During off season

repair the boat and the nets –

no fish in dry dock.

180.

Japanese farmers

turning bitter persimmons

into sweet candy.

181.

Mister Stock Market

will take from the fidgety

and give to patient.

182.

Fallen tree in creek

wood ducks paddling through branches

one follows the next.

183.

Woodpecker taps beat

hollow tree perfect log drum

flies away screeching.

Haiku Avenue

184.

Full moon over beach

breaking waves crash then go back.

We collect fire wood.

185.

Train roaring north bound

closed box cars painted clown red.

Where are the hobos?

186.

Old black plumb tree sighs

leaves falling in November

resting for the Spring.

187.

Civility cup

what would we do without tea

chance to have a talk.

188.

Cup of green wisdom

tea in morning brings wakeup

calming energy.

189.

Opening front door

morning paper on front porch

peaceful gray ground fog.

Haiku Avenue

190.

Cranes in wet rice field

playing songs with fragile flutes

winged ballerinas.

191.

Small snowflakes falling

slowly covering pine trees

blue jay turns his head.

192.

Dead bird on sidewalk

alley cat finds tasty meal

feathers blow away.

Robert Hobkirk

193.

Glorious Friday

freedom from grind starts tonight

popcorn and movie.

194.

Orange pumpkins and squash

left in the garden to rot –

open my blue eyes.

195.

Bird falls off tree branch

boy has a new bb gun

he dies a little.

196.

Dog panting after

chasing deer in snow blizzard

snow flake melts on tongue.

197.

Grumpy stink beetle

white cat bats it only once

does not have to run.

198.

Dead four point mule deer

laid out in back of pickup

no stopping at bar.

199.

Old leather wallet

held together with duct tape

dependable friend.

200.

Warm pile of deer guts

magpies, buzzards and ravens

deer season provides.

201.

Turtle neck sweater

misty rain beads and hangs on

walk to coffee shop.

202.

Sudden cold darkness

hail bouncing off concrete slab

raku kiln roaring.

203.

Tree trimmers climbing

chain saws cutting through dead limbs

no mourning for loss.

204.

Single loon on lake

black and white feathers, red eyes

dives and disappears.

205.

Burnt over black ground

quail picking seeds on ashes

calling chi-ca-go.

206.

Listen for bull frogs,

but I hear only silence

no tadpoles in Spring.

207.

Walmart shopping cart

used to get groceries home

abandoned in creek.

Haiku Avenue

208.

Oil tankers anchored

holds filled with crude to the brim

market ebbs and floods.

209.

Raining hard today

sparrows have found their shelter

blackberry bushes.

210.

Some beautiful things

I'll never forget the nest

five blue robin eggs.

211.

Love Christmas shopping

internet makes it easy

stores make it Christmas.

212.

Forgetting trash cans

neighbor puts them out for us

back and forth favors.

213.

Books stacked by my bed

rainy days welcome reading

television off.

214.

Hanging persimmons

arthritic naked branches

bright orange polka dots.

215.

After heavy rain

perfume bottle tipped over

smell the earth's fragrance.

216.

Caterpillar worms

stripping new leaves off branches

wait 'til birds find them.

217.

Walk along the creek

past the old railroad trestle

you will find turtles.

218.

T.V. football game

mostly women in the church

men rest on Sunday.

219.

Tall black cormorants

standing on barren branches -

black-robed priests on steps.

220.

Texas oil boom town

prepares for the bust to come

packed pickup trucks leave.

221.

Without marching band

ants travel in single file

not one out of step.

222.

Good cup of hot tea

an interesting novel

turn on light, close door.

223.

Two river otters

doing water somersaults,

playing or working?

224.

Old barren pear tree

all the leaves have fallen off

my children left home.

225.

Your fortune cookie

closest one on the small plate

don't take the wrong one.

Haiku Avenue

226.

Sack full of walnuts

smashing hard shell with hammer

all had small white worms.

227.

Morning is sunny

tree trimmers sharpen their saws

sign of coming storm.

228.

Huge Pacific storm

strange birds blown in from afar

sea birds over fields.

229.

Tangerines ripen

last night's rain washed the green leaves

sweet fruit, drab winter.

230.

Camping in winter

wake up to fresh fallen snow

smell the fresh coffee.

231.

Hoe winter garden

easy weeding in wet ground

onions, garlic sprout.

232.

Pile of raked brown leaves

mulch pile shrinks in constant rain

hear pitter-patter.

233.

Crowded coffee shop

loud chatter rises and falls

rain pours down outside.

234.

Two share umbrella

watch out for one inch puddles

both have wet shoulders.

235.

Drowned rat in dog's pool

floating face down near the side

rat trap shrugs shoulders.

236.

Plum tree stands alone

this morning snow fell lightly

white snow on black branch.

237.

Gray granite boulders

winter rains running in stream

snow silently falls.

Haiku Avenue

238.

Snow storm in mountains

drought ends, lakes full in summer

cows feed, calves will drink.

239.

Green pines and blue spruce

day after day heavy snow

forest fades in white.

240.

Underneath house eave

bird nest made of twigs and mud

vacant, abandoned.

241.

Together we walk

over sand dunes to the beach

waves whisper, "hush...hush."

242.

After the night's storm

absolute calm with blue sky

crow talking to self.

243.

Dozen Holstein cows

standing in mud, chewing cud

black and white puddles.

Haiku Avenue

244.

One table over

she looks at me with a smile

her boyfriend sits down.

245.

Cows walk through the muck

hooves in and out of the mud

earthy bedroom sounds.

246.

Thin layer of mud

spread out across the dirt path

foot prints follow me.

247.

Clusters of green seeds

turning red then falling black

pepper tree on trail.

248.

Under green shadows

dirt path leads to gas station

doughnuts and coffee.

249.

Head full of worry

ocean wave music calms mind

healing flood drowns I.

250.

Black swan flying in

bread loaf sold for a penny

lake of burning oil.

251.

Financial turmoil

tanker crashes on Wall Street

prices plunge lower.

252.

Fog rolling over

green hills onto silent bay

gray horse nods his head.

Robert Hobkirk

253.

Message in bottle

sea treasure after big storm

haiku from Japan.

254.

Choppy trading day

close short position, small change

long anxiety.

255.

Crow rests on scarecrow

seeds fall out of rotting squash

Spring brings rain, squash sprouts.

Haiku Avenue

256.

Lying down I rest

white clouds travel through blue sky

hawk circles above.

257.

Boy fishing cold stream

knows every rock, every log

summer vacation.

258.

No trespassing sign

geese fly in with black feet down

hungry for new grass.

259.

Blue morning glories

climb up and over the fence

white paint peels off boards.

260.

Tired and weary

Salvation Army bell rings

coin clinks in kettle.

261.

Water runs down street

sprinklers swing over soaked lawn

long afternoon nap.

262.

A tall blonde coffee

table outside, nothing more

cell phones chatter noise.

263.

Hives buzz to Spring's drum

apple blossoms with arms wide -

farmer gets a loan.

264.

Friday night payday

tomato soup for our lunch

pizza for supper.

Robert Hobkirk

265.

Milk in glass bottles

heavy cream rises to top

bottles on door step.

266.

White blanket, not snow

pear blossoms paint the delta

black levee cuts through.

267.

Sturgeon running up

winter waters running down

sales up in bait shop.

Haiku Avenue

268.

Super sea tanker

big mountain slowly moving

water parts and fills.

269.

Coffee cup on roof

driver, passenger chit-chat

car leaves, coffee spills.

270.

When I was a boy

my bicycle had no lock

I walked through dark woods.

Robert Hobkirk

271.

Complaints spill over

old folks sit in doughnut shop

coffee maker drips.

272.

Clamming for pismos

wade past breakers to sand bar

sack clatters with clams.

273.

When night tide is right

grunions go ashore, plant eggs

frying pan sizzles.

Haiku Avenue

274.

Picking blackberries

two jars full for baking pies

rabbit hides in thorns.

275.

Blades turning over

rototiller working hard

worms can't run away.

276.

Buyer in hurry

depends on luck, not knowledge

fast cash runs away.

277.

Boiler room chatter

desperate people pitching

power fails – silence.

278.

Bagholder goes broke

market acts like jealous chimp

sad face gets ripped off.

279.

Something never seen

snail crawling across highway

failure at get-go.

280.

Orange pumpkins rotting

spilling out their guts and seeds

crows find wreck and feed.

281.

Owl hoots at sunset

lonely sounds and lonely sights

old woman alone.

282.

Road rage and cursing

man with violent hot temper –

graveyards are peaceful.

283.

Snow geese flying high

white specks strung out across sky

sound of barking dogs.

284.

Socks drying in sun

old man sitting on brick wall

peeling orange for lunch.

285.

Run hand over head

deep in imagination

ouch – pimple breaks spell.

286.

<u>I Ching</u>, other books

brown paper grocery bag full

can't eat cooking books.

287.

Feliz Navidad

selling tamales on the street

poor man's restaurant.

288.

How's your day so far?

Woke up grumpy once again -

shocking honest man.

289.

Perched on high bar stool

holidays disappoint some

morgue's busy season.

290.

Be a decent man

if you want a good woman

don't be an angel.

291.

In old New Orleans

no exit on Bourbon Street

party never stops.

292.

Night before Christmas

dads are busy with wrenches

bicycles with bows.

293.

Necessary lies

Santa ate all the cookies

the milk is gone too.

294.

Another Christmas

family dog gets tasty scraps

recycle bin full.

Robert Hobkirk

295.

Cold north blast comes in

price of natural gas sinks

gas bill still stays high.

296.

Long running shadows

playing tag in orange moonlight

catch me if you can.

297.

Wild California

black walnuts in light green husks

dusty from Summer.

298.

Sitting in Starbucks

lyrical haiku rasta

coffee stains paper.

299.

Cigarette filter

dipped in coffee and ashes

painting on napkin.

300.

Gnarly black plum tree

soft white blossoms fall to ground

later purple fruit.

301.

Texting with one hand

balancing toddler on hip

kung fu motherhood.

302.

Carpenter's pencil

square, level, rule, and chalk line

honest profession.

303.

Shabby neighborhood

new snow hides dreary street scene

warm weather brings slush.

304.

Dog barking up tree

squirrel chattering down his taunts

last leaf on tree falls.

305.

Old skinny woman

herds two cows down muddy path

cow bell swings slow beat.

306.

Insect falls off twig

swims on top of dark water

bass rising splashes.

307.

Oranges freeze on tree

my old dog Belle sleeps curled up

heater hums all night.

308.

High electric lines

pass over fields with new grass

cattle graze all day.

309.

Every hot summer

orange butterfly in back yard

cannot be same one.

Haiku Avenue

310.

Brown moth in bath tub

confused, all it sees is white

wings rap enamel.

311.

Inside fancy store

rich woman pays for mink coat

outside, bag lady.

312.

Remember summer

blue dragonflies hovering

squadron over pond.

313.

Haiku comes in night

get out of warm cozy bed

find pen and paper.

314.

Squeaky wheel gets greased

driver thinks got to replace

new wheel is quiet.

315.

Outside Starbucks shop

panhandler begs for small change

teeth chattering "please."

316.

Two women walking

there is silence between them

something is broken.

317.

New Year's Day morning

wake up without hangover

sober year ahead.

318.

Full Chinese New Year

firecrackers and red dragons

ducks hanging in shop.

319.

Sipping oolong tea

pulling fortunes from cookies

monkey and dragon.

320.

Tea from the far East

Coca Cola from Georgia

coffee from Brazil.

321.

Pair of metal legs

soldier coming home from war

wife not at airport.

322.

Sun glare on water

a mallard drake turns his head

green flashes on-off.

323.

Raft of dead cattails

great white heron stands on top

slow lift off, legs up.

324.

Black fish net nylons

a tear just below her skirt

dog is told to sit.

325.

For some weird reason

I feel safe on a jet plane

nervous city walk.

326.

Woman sweeps sidewalk

straw broom chases away leaves

crawling snail leaves trail.

327.

Almond tree blossomed

biting artic frost came down

flowers froze in night.

Haiku Avenue

328.

Friends may refuse you

your dog always walks with you

sometimes he won't fetch.

329.

Black cat crossed my path

it will not bring me bad luck

cat had one white leg.

330.

New resolution

today much fat will be lost

next week found again.

331.

Under the surface

orange koi swimming in green pond

cat dips her black paw.

332.

Bread on the water

fish in the pond dash over

water boils then calm.

333.

Ocean reflects sky

world fades on vanishing point

we always look out.

About the Author

Robert Hobkirk lives with his lovely wife Jeannine and their two dogs, Molly and Belle, in Northern California. Besides family and friends, he enjoys nature, the arts, and baseball on the radio. He looks for art in the ordinary, that which is taken for granted. He posts an art blog at http://hobkirkartblog.blogspot.com/.

Printed in Great Britain
by Amazon.co.uk, Ltd.,
Marston Gate.